The Trilogy

One Human's Evolution Through Poetry

MARILYN MORRISON

BALBOA.PRESS

A DIVISION OF HAY HOUSE

Balboa Press books may be ordered through booksellers or by contacting:

Balboa Press
A Division of Hay House
1663 Liberty Drive
Bloomington, IN 47403
www.balboapress.com
844-682-1282

Print information available on the last page.

ISBN: 978-1-9822-7171-8 (sc)
ISBN: 978-1-9822-7172-5 (e)

Balboa Press rev. date: 07/21/2021

This book of poetry is dedicated to all the people,
and there have been many, who taught me to think,
to question, and to be honest with myself.

I am blessed to have had so many Angels in
my life. And to my daughters, who have been
my inspiration from their very first breath.

Contents

Part I: Reflections
Thoughts and Ideas from a Common Life 1993 - 2000

Part II: Enter the Divine
Poems from Another Place and Time 2010 - 2013

Part III: Awake, Alert, Alive 2013 – Present

Elegy:

Social Ambiguity:

Preface

This book is a collection of poetry written from 1993 through 2020. Each section was created based on my journey to understand myself, my life, and my spiritual path.

Sometimes written in desperation, sometimes with careful thought, and other times with humor. Every decade brought me closer to a deeper understanding through drawing, singing, and poetry.

My life has become a labor of love to myself, my journey, and my understanding of humanity so I can put the past behind me and work toward peace for myself and others.

Over the years I have studied bodywork, yoga, Tai Chi, and many other forms of therapy, including talk therapy. However, I believe my artful heart was always the instigator of learning and desire to reach above for a deeper look at my own humanness.

I hope you enjoy these poems and allow them to speak to you as well. In the end, we are simply human beings struggling to reach a peaceful and satisfying life while at the same time allowing each of us to share our personal journey with others.

Introduction

In my fiftieth year, as part of an intense three-year soul-searching journey that altered my life completely, I set out on a path of healing my heart. After graduating from Kennesaw State College with a degree in Communications, I decided the corporate environment was not for me. Following my heart into many therapies, I decided to go to Colorado and study the bodywork of Dr. Ida P. Rolf. This awareness, of not only my own body, but that of my clients led me to a path I could not have anticipated. Bodywork practice led me to yoga which in turn led me to teacher training. Yoga led me to meditation and eventually to India.

The journey back into my heart has been a 25-year journey from the outside world to the inner world of my heart and soul...After singing in a rock n' roll band in the nineties, I started writing poetry. Writing became my therapy, a way of trying to understand my life.

It was 1993, and I was in a relationship that I believed could result in marriage. I dreamed of marrying him in the backyard or in a small chapel, but somehow, the dream never materialized. After about eight years and with the end of the relationship, I became acutely aware of the fact that I needed to focus on my numerous inner contradictions. I thought poetry would be a good venue for exploration, a way to connect and communicate with myself. The poems in *Part I Reflections: Thoughts and Ideas from a Common Life* are simple ones. In their simplicity, I began to open to a more spiritual way of seeing myself and my relationship to a larger reality, as I searched for my higher self. Feeling strong and confident, I left the relationship in 2002 and with a business partner's help, started Harmony Yoga.

Part II Enter the Divine: Poems from Another Place and Time was written during a period of my life when I was involved in a very intense relationship. That deep feeling of love took me to another level of understanding. Even though the relationship only lasted for about one and a half years, it left a huge imprint on my heart. A broken heart is a great teacher. The relationship didn't last, but my truth became more real to me, more real than anyone else could have taught me. I will always be grateful for that time.

Sometimes learning is painful, but I found a part of myself I was not aware of before, a deep connection to my inner SELF. That's why this section is called *Enter the Divine*. Some of these poems may even speak to your own relationship experiences.

Between *Part II: Enter the Divine* and *Part III: Awake, Alert, Alive,* there is a period about four years. During that time, I closed my yoga studio and began working in an addiction and mental health issues recovery center. This new chapter in my life opened and inspired me to finding ways to understand the problem of addiction, using yoga and meditation classes effectively, and teaching relaxation as a support to aid recovery.

I began to see that my issues and their issues were not so different. The bond that I developed with the recovery center students was one I had not experienced with the students in the yoga studio. It was just different. I could relate to their struggles with recovery. It also helped me realize that struggle is simply a part of life that needs to be recognized and acknowledged.

I am forever grateful to those students for helping me open up even more to understanding the spiritual path and its importance in our lives. We may not completely understand how the Spiritual energy supports our humanness, but we can acknowledge for ourselves that struggle is a natural part of personal growth. In this way, we can learn from our decisions and grow from our mistakes.

You never know what Spirit has in store for you until you find yourself in a place you did not orchestrate yourself. A place where life just happened, finding yourself in a new experience, with the challenges we need to support healthy change. I have learned more from my students than they have learned from me. One important lesson: the teacher should always be open to learning from their student.

Reflections

Thoughts and Ideas
from a Common Life

1993 - 2000

Can you imagine?

What ideas could you expound or share
that might lift a world out of despair?
Are there words you could express
that might change this feeling of hopelessness?

A message that would help all nations see
the answer lies in compassion and empathy?
If we are willing to see that we are all affected
by the simple fact that we are all connected.

We might set aside our fear and grief
to move beyond in one united belief
that our imagined separateness could cease
And we could open the door to global peace.

The Creation of You

What you make of yourself will surely be
exactly what the universe is waiting to see.
So step right up, don't wait or linger,
make a wish and lift your finger.
Your beaming light will make you shine,
all you need is to take your time.
Just decide within your heart your
intention is the place to start. Go
ahead, test it now,
Ask for something, wait, and WOW!

I Won the Lottery

When all those tiny little sperm
Swimming upstream with much concern,
Were searching for that Special Egg
Of which they could partake.
How lucky you see,
That they happened to be
In just the right place
For them to interface.
Thus, starting an undertaking,
Barely nine months in the making.
Now from where I stand,
I turned out to be
The winner of the Egg-Sperm lottery.

Perfection

Before we had thoughts, we had feelings galore,
Before we began the long arduous chore
Of judging and qualifying in all of our waking,
Thinking Perfection was ours for the making.
Our task is much easier than you can guess.

We need to use our senses more and heads less.
Nature provided all we'll ever require,
It's here for the taking if we desire.
We're already Perfect if we could only see,
We don't have to do, we just have to BE.

Our Beautiful Female Body

As I am looking through the Victoria's Secret Catalogue,
I notice a very interesting analog.
There seems to be a slight discrepancy
between what Mother Nature gave to them and to me.
I am a person who loves a good challenge
So I set out to see if I could come up with the knowledge
to solve one of the greatest mysteries,
And find out more information if you please,
On how women so thin became so well endowed.
A quandary of such magnitude it is covered in shroud.
To my shock and surprise some of these women implanted
Saline and what not and granted
Someone the permission to open the spaces,
and cut their bodies right under their faces.
To insert some sort of alien object,
To go from an A to a C cup, I find more than suspect.
In the breast development stages I may have been slow,
But at least in my mind I am smart enough to know
how totally boring it would be
If we all lost our individuality.
And somehow by some fluke in our family tree,
we all wind up looking just like Barbie.
Anatomically we would be in grave danger forever.
There is no way our parts could fit together.
We might possibly be able to talk,
But none of us would have the ability to walk.

Now I feel more than gifted,
Knowing that a burden has been lifted
And taken away any demand on my part
To try to perfect a work of art.
We don't have to improve on Mother Nature,
Perfection was programmed into the female creature.

Nature

I love walking
In the woods. Sometimes I Stop,
look up at the trees. I stand
Very still and look at their swaying tops.
All moving in unison, in rhythm with each other.
I feel my body start to sway with them and I become
One with the motion, the flow, the breeze. I feel the Freedom of the
trees letting Mother Nature fold them Together one into the other. I
feel folded with them.
This movement,
This freedom,
This motion, Is this
What Heaven
is all About?

A Poem for Donna

I wasn't sure my being here had any reason
Until you were born early that fall season.
The way my life would change I did not comprehend,
Even as I held your tiny body in my hand.
But a place of longing I had been aware of
Suddenly disappeared and I was filled with love.
Little did I know how my life would turn,
Or how profoundly from you I would learn.
I had no idea those labor pains were just the beginning
Of the growing pains we would both be experiencing.
I wanted to teach you to live a life you could value,
But I learned more from you than I could ever tell you.
I learned that becoming a Mother
Meant opening to receive love from another.
My growing pains in those early days
Come from my inability to understand your loving ways.
When you reached your thirteenth year,
A mirror of myself become painfully clear.
In your innocence you reflected my rage.
I began to see I had us both locked in a cage.
You forced me to grow and release my past,
I was so afraid your love for me wouldn't last.
I knew when you left me, I would be alone again.
My life without you, I could not comprehend.
The lesson you taught me as no one else could
Was the importance of letting go, then I understood;
Love isn't real unless you can let go.

It is freedom that enables a child to grow.
I thank you, Donna, for showing me love is the key,
And unlocking the cage so we could both be free
To finish our journey as daughter and mother,
Sharing our love and appreciation for each other.

The Office Party

I was once invited to an office mixer,
As you might imagine there was plenty of elixir.
I was bored as could be
Because I don't drink you see,
And office politics can be
The most boring thing in the world to me.
All of a sudden, I happened to glance
And out of the corner of my eye there stood Lance.
A man so handsome, lean and trim,
With a gaggle of women all around him.
Of course, I tried not to notice his incredible bod
Then he glanced over at me and gave me a nod.
What did that mean, was he looking for a fling?
That smile on his face could mean only one of two things,
Either he's gloating over all the woman he's found
Or he thinks I might be the one to lay him down.
I'm not quite familiar with the rules of this game,
It has been so long since I played it, I feel quite lame.
You see, I was up at 3am and could sleep no more,
My baby had a fever, needing medicine from the store
Then the six-year-old got up, ready for the day.
I looked and daylight was still hours away.
So, nod if you must, if your ego it feeds,
But as for me, a couple of hours of sleep is all I need.

I Can Fly

As I was walking in the woods one day
Feeling quite cheerful and yearning to play,
I began asking my angel for some help and guidance
But all I got was deafening silence.
I wondered why no words of wisdom came to me,
But then as I looked, THEY were there to see.
Right behind my shoulders and just above my head,
Were a magnificent pair of wings trimmed in bright red,
Filled with the most extraordinary colors I've ever seen,
Swirling, gold, yellow, orange, and green.
They were definitely wings from an other-worldly creature.
They were arched high, that was their most spectacular feature,
They looked like no wings I had seen on a bird or animal,
I couldn't believe they were designed for a mammal.
My angel guide said they looked as they should.
Then a light breeze that began at my feet,
Swirled me around, I felt the ground retreat.
A light gust of wind whisked me up high,
I was frightened at first, I didn't know I could fly.
I took a deep breath and released a sigh,
When I looked over my shoulder, I saw a dove flying by.
As I left my cares and worries behind,
I wondered why it took so long for me to find
This amazing gift that was mine for the taking.
I guess it required a little awakening.

And then in one tremendous and heavenly motion,
My wings opened wide and I had the notion
That I could let go of all earthly things
And totally rely on my angel wings,
To soar from high above and see
What a glorious feeling it is to be FREE.

When I Was Young

When I was young, I was desperately in need
Of a movement trend that would teach me to lead.
So I spent my life reaching up,
Trying to fill a half empty cup.
But then bracing myself, trying to stall
What inevitably became a long spiraling fall.
As I've grown older what I have learned,
Chasing what I think I have earned,
Spending some time in the middle ground,
Where I can be still and hear the spirit sound.
Giving me guidance on how to proceed,
Learning how to follow instead of trying to lead.

Ask for What You Want

Your intention is who you are
So decide upfront to be a STAR.
Stand up tall and make it clear
What you want is very near.
Don't waste time on petty things,
Raise your voice and make it sing.
Make no mistake you will attract
What you give will come back.
What you want lies deep inside
Only YOU have to power to provide
So aim high and shine your light
All great things are within your sight.

A Poem for Anne

Here's a very small gift I hope will convey
A message to you in a VERY big way.
Your friendship has been so easily given,
I'm starting to believe that one reason I am living
Is just to learn about friendship from someone like you,
Who has helped make a dream of mine come true.

Now that's real friendship in my book,
This chapter of my life has made me look
More closely at what is of real value,
And then find a way in which to tell you.
Thanks for being there and sharing with me
The gift of your voice as we make our HISTORY.

Anne was a friend who helped me start a chanting group in 1998.
We had loads of fun with it.
(She later married and moved to Oregon.)

The Creative Channel

One day I had the impression
That I needed a format for my artful expression.
But I never expected the day to come
When my dendrites and axons would force me to run
Straight to the computer, and begin to enter
A thought or idea gushing straight from my center.
Ideas twisting and swirling with such force,
They could push a tornado right off its course.
At times I'll begin doing some domestic chore,
Something as mindless as mopping the floor.
And then as if the words that inspire
Have become a dragon breathing fire,
I must rush to write them down as fast as I can
And extinguish the flame before it kindles again.
When you read these poems, I am sure you'll agree,
Instead of owning my words, they seem to own me.
But my thoughts transport me from my everyday space
Into an opening where no limits or boundaries take place.
A space where ideas and thoughts can soar,
And my creative voice can release its mighty roar.

The Things We Do

The things we do day by day
Create this game of life we play.
And in every want or need or deed,
There is a quest, a vision that proceeds.
There's a driving force, a wave we ride,
Making its way to low or high tide.
But the flow and ebb will intimately bring
Whatever energy is moving "THE THING."

Learning to Love Myself

I feel as though I have fallen madly in love,
Because I have every symptom you can think of.
The dizziness, the giddiness, I am even absent-minded,
But I have no fear that my love will be unrequited.
All my symptoms are simply a part
Of a sense of wellbeing and the opening of my heart.
Perhaps it is the time of the year that is causing me to see
Myself as a part of the great and loving infinity.
My lover is myself, the reflection of my dual nature,
My male and female in a loving embrace with each other.
I feel as if a marriage has taken place
Inside my being, my own sacred space.
What a wonderful Christmas gift I have received,
To feel this love for myself instead of need.
This vast resource of love I can openly share,
In connection with all just from being aware.

Finding Enlightenment

For a long time there has been a great argument
As my left and right brain seem to lament.
One side says, "Be still, you need to be intuiting."
While the other side says, "You need to be doing."
I want to do but I also want to be,
I have trouble finding the middle road you see.
I've heard for years that balance is the answer,
This message come to me from all the great masters.
Deepak, Wayne, even the Dalai Lama have told me,
And I want to follow in the footsteps of "His Most Holy."
But who does their washing, shopping, and walking the dog?
How do they find time for their daily jog?
What is this ordinary woman to do?
When I sit down, I just begin to stew.
Why don't I have ten minutes to rest?
Am I being put to some ridiculous test?
To see if perhaps I can figure it out,
How to get to the end of my life and shout,
"I did it….I am FREE!"
No more dishes to wash for me.
I'm ascending to heaven and now I have time
To leisurely lie around on Cloud Nine.

Christmas IS Home

Why are we searching to find a place
Looking outside of the human race?
What we need is deep inside
In the comfortable home where we reside.
This heart space in the physical body we call home
Is there to access when we feel lost and alone.
Next time you feel caught up in the race
Sit still and recall that heart-home place.
For home is the place where compassion lives
The place where we know what it is to give.
Give something of yourself this Christmas season
And you will discover a very good reason.
To awaken your heart and your ability to win
This human race we find ourselves running in.

Beginning of Life

It strikes me as rather curious
That my life has somehow become so serious.
From such a relaxing and meager start
With my only focus the beat of a heart.
There was a time when I had no awareness
Of matters that strained my sense of fairness.
To be blessed in such a protected space,
With no need to question my rightful place.
All felt beautifully arranged in a glorious plan,
I needed nothing to be but who I am.
My host was perfect in every way,
We share a give and take day by day.
But then as time stretched out before me,
I heard an alien sound I could not foresee.
It had a rhythm, a movement in and then out,
Something expanding and contraction no doubt.
I was sure I had the equipment to do this,
But somehow something was strangely amiss.
A pact with my host I did not understand,
Somehow part of the master plan as the weeks went by,
This comfortable place, once so heavenly,
Now seemed to be closing in on me.
It's a wonder to this day I can ever trust,
Because then with a pulsing and mighty thrust,
I was cast out of my heavenly bubble
With the sense that this moment might mean trouble.
How huge my world had grown to be,
From my humble beginnings as a tiny seed.
Now that I have had fifty odd years to reap,

I can finally say it was worth the leap,
But as I sit here and start to ponder
The next transition, I cannot help but wonder,
Would it be advantageous for me to know,
How many of these seeds I have to sow.
For now, a new question is opening my heart,
Is this the end of my journey, or a brand-new start?

Me

When I was a
child of eight
years I was
playing with my
doll, I was
sitting
in front of my mother. I was showing her what I needed
as I hugged and caressed "my little baby." She didn't pay any
attention to me. She was watching TV. I got angry, I needed
something. I shook my doll so hard
her arm fell off in my hand.
At that moment, I understood
sadness and guilt, and
I clearly Understood what it
feels like to   be invisible.
I took my doll   to the attic
where I could   piece her back
together.   A question
arose that   day. Where
was this empty   Place coming
from and   how would
I ever fill   myself up?

What I Learned from a Snowflake

Looking with wondering eyes to the sky,
I see tiny white snowflakes come drifting by,
Each floating to earth from their heavenly place,
I watch in awe at their peaceful race.
So unobtrusive and quiet as they descend,
With no awareness of where their journey will end.
They fall unconcerned about where they will land,
Knowing Mother Earth will gently hold out her hand.
As they transition to water to nourish us all,
And realize this purpose is part of their call.
I'm taking a lesson from these snowflakes I've seen,
To let life guide me and be more serene.
Because if I never find peace in my silent being,
I might end up not even seeing,
How essential those moments of stillness can be,
For the reflection and evolution of the INNER ME.

The Importance of Solitude

I wander on my path alone.
What do I have to fear?
Aloneness–loneliness–oneness–solitude–separation
No, this is my choice.
At times I choose solitude,
This quiet helps me touch my most inner places,
Allowing my internal voice to be heard.
I awaken in the silence,
my spirit guides me on the path
of connectedness to the "all"
and to the "nothing at all."

Why Am I Here?

I must feel my connection to the
Inner most…the core of the Earth
I must feel my connection
to the Outer most…the Earth Plane
And see my physical body as a temporary host.
Now I understand the full spectrum of life.
Through the core of my body, as the conductor
Of the spiritual energy
In this magnificent stream, I can flow forever.
Here lies my connection with my infinite SELF.
This connection frees me from the fear of death
And my temporary life on Earth
And encourages me to ask the question,
"What is my role here in the Evolution
of the human creature?" That is what I seek.
That is what I long to know.
That is what my life here on Earth is all about.

Life's Decisions

All of life's choices bring with them special challenges.
It is not about being single. It is not about being married.
It is not about being divorced. It is about being content with
Our own masculine/feminine energy...
There are no mistakes,
Only Divine opportunities for learning to Love.
Whether you are single, married, divorced,
Life is always showing us what we need to see.
Will you see? Will you accept the challenge and face your true
LOVING SELF?
Single life will show you how to focus on yourself. Bringing
fewer distractions, more time for inner contemplation. This can
be a special time for awareness of SELF.
A partner will push your buttons of imbalance.
Bring about discord and at times intense feelings.
A partner is a life guide to help our issues surface for healing.
That is what they are meant to do...
So use your single time wisely, this is an important life lesson.
See your partner as a gift for healing a wounded past.
Live your life as if you asked for it, as if you are co-creating it.
This precious time is the gift that you created to help you find your
LOVING SELF.

Follow the Natural Way

When the wind takes a turn and swells all must obey.
The birds do not try to fly against the wind,
They position themselves so the wind can lift them and
Make their flight easier.
The trees do no fight for control with the breeze.
Each branch, each leaf, gives in to Mother Nature's movement.
So, we too must allow the winds of change
to help guide our direction.
To resist is to struggle against our innate nature.
This Creates stress and discord in our being.
There is Heavenly bliss awaiting those who follow their
natural instincts.
This is the survival plan,
Our humanness uniting with our soul
for the purpose of total Harmony.

I Can Dream

There's only one place I'd rather be,
On the other side of world in Tahiti.
Whenever I feel stressed and all dragged out,
Instead of having a martini or scream and shout,
I get this crazy notion
That somewhere over there beside the ocean,
Swaying in the breeze,
There is a little grass shack beckoning to me.
Ah, a couple of days on the beach,
With the surf in my ear and my hand out to reach
For a glass of coconut milk, brought to me
By a native boy sitting by my knee,
Fanning my body with palm leaves,
He looks remarkably like Keanu Reeves.
He knows that I'm stressed and wants to do
Whatever it will take to make UNBLUE.
But then from out of nowhere I hear a pop,
The sound of my bubble breaking, trying to stop
My imagination from going too far,
That I grab my purse and head for my car,
to hop on a plane that will carry me
Across the ocean to my destiny.

Mother's Day Poem

How many years did I spend making beds, doing dishes,
mopping floors, and cooking meals?
How many years picking up clothes, bandaging hurts
sleeping lightly in case someone needed me?
I was so busy doing, there were days when I
scarcely knew if anyone was home.
I had finally mastered my JOB.
You grew older and required less attention.
I could get the cooking, cleaning done without feeling
totally exhausted.
One day I looked around to see who needed me
and everyone was gone.
It's not that I expected fanfare or accolades or a
thank you every day.
I loved caring for you, I truly loved making a home for you,
but I realized when you left, you never said "Good-bye."
I just looked around and you were gone.
I miss you. Some days I can still see you in my mind's eye,
sleeping, playing, laughing or crying.
I still feel the need to nurture you,
please keep me in your heart, as you are forever in mine.

Enter the Divine

Poems from Another Place and Time

2010 - 2013

Rainy Day

A damp, cool, rainy afternoon,
rain washing and cleansing the air.
The earth recycling, rivers, lakes, and oceans,
renewing Mother Earth one small drop at a time.
Watching nature with her unbending intent to renew
brings me to stillness,
I become a passive observer to nature's cleansing process,
each drop falls, hits the earth and spatters to hundreds of
smaller drops.
As I watch each drop, I feel each splatter in the depth of my being.
My cells begin bumping against each other in excitement,
celebrating this beautiful rainy day.
My inner being feels cleansed.
I am reminded of the intense vibration in all of nature, all of life,
a smile breaks my lips.
In the cleansing face of a rainy day clearing all stress away,
my awareness turns to you, my love.
Reminding me what is most important to me today.
Love for God and the person God put directly in my path to
change my life forever.

And God Said

Look, I know you want to be alone in your misery,
but I have a better plan.

I said, Misery? I am not in misery.

God said, No?
I sent you a personal invitation to be with me,
and what do I get as a response? Sobbing.
Why do you feel so lost?
You wander searching, you flounder, flopping wildly on the dock
trying to find your way back into the sea of Love,
I am trying to remove the dock, the wall that separates you from me,
and you sob?
Open your heart, open your eyes, open your mind.
You are brilliant, you are mine,
you are all that separates the world from Divine Love.
Guess what…you are holding up the process.
Your heart is the key that will unlock the door
for humanity to enter heaven on Earth,
why do you resist me?

I am afraid, I answer.

You are afraid?
You live in separation and that does not frighten you? God said.
My glorious plan lies right in front of you and you won't take the one
step with your intention to be with me forever,
because you are afraid of my Divine Love?

You could think about this for a moment or two
and tell me if that makes sense to you.

If I take the step…if I dive into your Divine Presence,
what will be left of ME?
I am afraid to disappear, to lose myself, I said.

God said, you are lost now,
I am sending you a lifeline to Divine Eternity,
your ego is all you have to surrender, I created you,
my Divine Plan manifested your life for this moment in the time line
so you could make the decision with your own free will to join me in
heaven on earth and complete your purpose here.
I am offering you eternal salvation,
and you are worried about your ego?
You might want to consider that choice.
What has your life brought you that is so precious that you withhold
your LOVE from ME?
You could think about this for a moment or two
and tell me if that makes sense to you.

I have a beautiful life, I said.
I have everything, a wonderful…amazing family,
a business that gives my life purpose, a relationship that fills me,
my artful heart. What else is there.
I must hold onto my life, or I might lose it.

God chuckled, literally, I hear God chuckling.
Then he said, lose it, you will lose it, it is imperative that you lose it.
I gave you all that, those were my gifts to you.
Did you think for one minute you manifested that life on your own?

You really are living in your ego if that is the case.

I wanted you. I wanted you with me.

I showed you the power of my love with your children, your business, and your relationship, your art,

which by the way is really beginning to reflect Me in a beautiful way.

Did you think that was it? I am just getting started with you. I know you cannot see beyond your own needs right now...

Humans are short sighted.

I designed you this way.

You are not supposed to see the whole plan...if you did, you might want to come to me too soon before you are finished here.

Look...I realize I am asking a lot...I am asking that you trust ME.

Trust that I know who you are better than you know yourself.

I know your heart.

I created you in my image, remember?

And then God smiled because he knew
that I knew he made perfect sense.

God's Shifting Sands

The body like shifting sand, energy…moving, coursing,
Sometimes halting, sometimes racing, keeping up, laying behind,
Balancing, staggering like an hourglass on its side
Rocking back and forth.
The sand always moving, always seeking equilibrium.

This is God's Divine Plan,
God's Magnificent Plan.
Like a giant pendulum, swinging us away,
then swing us back again.

Where is the solid ground today?
None to be found.
Our choices, our free will exhausted,
God has taken the helm for today.
The great healer anticipates our movement,
filling us with the Almighty force, the great leveler,
The Holy Spirit.
This is God's work,

Creating Master Pieces of each and every one.
Moving us sometimes gently like a breeze,
sometimes more forcefully like a raging storm,
back towards the original design.
To live in balance with Divine Love.

Last Night

Last night you came to me in the wee hours of the morning.
Touching your flame of love to my heart,
searing and burning your way inside.

Making sense of love is like trying to fly with a granite ball
the size of Earth tethered to the ankles.

The yearning, ever present, to stare into your eyes
for a reassuring glimpse of Forever,
is the soul's immediate longing.

No mercy granted, no forgiveness tonight.
The dark night of the soul keeps illumination at bay.
Can you tell me, just a small hint, of the atrocity I committed
that has reduced my heart to smoldering ash?

Ah, I FEEL the answer vibrating in every cell of my body...FEAR
Fear that our love was an unrealistic fantasy
or is it fear that our love will manifest our wildest dreams?
Freewill can be a loathsome responsibility.

As day breaks over the horizon, I ask myself,
"What would be good for breakfast this morning?
A little unrealistic love over easy,

OR

a wild dream whipped into action?"
Hmmm, Just another challenging day.

My World, Our World

My World
Meditate, contemplate, differentiate, alleviate
Words with purpose,
Welcome to my world.
The world of the straightforward.
The narrow path,
Not because venturing off the path is wrong,
but because leaving the path blurs the focus.

For years, this is ME.

Our World
One day there is two,
No longer me alone, but me and you.
Two magnifies reality exponentially in every shared moment,
in every shared thought, in every shared awareness.

The eyes reveal a new world awaiting exploration,
exploring bodies, hearts…melding together,
Coming apart, the great adventure of lovers,
sipping from the wine glass of love,
Struggling to quench the thirst of a thousand years.

Now the focus on two in one shared reality,
all else tedious and strained
lives only living to come back together,
lives circling each other, enveloping, caressing each other.

What else is there? What else needs to be?
Living from one passionate embrace to another,
the point of focus...NOW

Coming together because the magnetic energy insists on it,
to fight it would be ludicrous, even sinful...
Surrender the only option, the sensible way.
Longing, yearning, passion,
the attraction of two souls yet to be defined
honoring the force that brings them together
to know each other's heart,
staring into eternity with every breath.

The Organic Gardener

We are all growing gardens by planting seeds...our thoughts.
This is an internal garden, the garden which affects our internal energy.
What do you want to see growing in your garden?

There are many thought packets.
Every possible seed packet is available to us.
In this case the seeds that grow discontent and pain are all
very expensive. They will cost you your life.
They will grow rotten fruit and weeds...nothing more.

And yet we continue to plant these seeds...
these harmful thoughts every day.
Disillusionment, Resentment, Fear,
Unforgiving Heart, Disappointment, all come at a very high cost
to the evolution the human spirit.
Since the body is the reflection of the spirit...these seeds create dis-ease.
Using these packets, we begin to die a slow, painful death.
Love, Acceptance, Beauty, Faith, Compassion, Encouragement, all
FREE. These seeds plant the tree of life. With Fruitful abundance.
This fruit is healing for the body, mind and spirit.
We have a choice. We always have a proactive choice.
There is no such thing as "just a word."
Every word has an energy,
each word represents something that "is being created" with words...
an energy being dispersed onto the planet.

Choose words carefully
in conversations with others and conversations with yourself.
Practice talking to yourself using kindness and compassion…
take those words out into the world, spread them freely.

Organic Gardening plants the seeds of God.
These seeds are living ideas, words that help humans grow…
grow and evolve toward our God nature.

When you plant these seeds, you are tilling and cultivating
God's garden. God's Garden allows all humans to
grow and develop naturally.

Will you help to feed the world…
Will you help to fuel the world with compassion and love…
God's love.
We can use our "God Speaks" voice and change the world.

The Autumn Equinox

The harvest moon, the star filled sky,
revealing the mysteries of the ancient worlds.
The sky opens up and shares its vast eternal
knowledge with those who are open to see.
Lying on a rock, faces turned towards the heavens.
The giant boulder, the bald man's head,
peeking out from Mother Earth.

We are Lying on his forehead, soaking up his
wisdom into our backs like a thirsty sponge.
The energy rising to meet the sky, and us,
faces to the Heavens, backs against the Earth,
lying caressed like the filling of a sandwich
between the bread of Mother Earth and Father Sky,
breathing in the air that blows like the winds of the north
across our faces, through our hair, along our skin.

The front of the body, heart and mind making a direct connection
with the Man in the Moon, Big Dipper,
even Jupiter is glowing like a huge star, magnificent.
The stars all twinkling, winking at us from above as if to say,
"Carry on you two lovers, carry on."

Heaven is at hand right here on Earth,
right now, in this very moment, love is everywhere,
love is eminent, love conquers all.
God is alive and well on planet Earth this evening, sending love
to all those who are willing to look up and live.
We are blessed beyond words.

The Child

Desperation, Anticipation,
Void, Fullness Traveling the journey
between the opposites,
Exhausting… all energy seeking balance.
The journey of TRUTH since early… childhood.
The inner child knows nothing but awareness.
All life is simply THAT.
Complete and total abandonment to THAT, no choice, no option.
Just the great WHAT IS.

How to make sense of something that cannot be spoken,
Even if it could…
who would dare drag those skeletons up from the depths.
The tears, sadness, yearning, the feeling,
that feeling that defies description.

The wanting for something other than what IS,
What does a child know of the world except what IS.
There IS no other.
God plants us where we can grow fruitful.
What to do when the garden is barren, unable to bear fruit.
Where does a child go for Solace, Comfort, Love,
What to do with the gnawing hunger,
The plate is full, but nothing satisfies,

The deep hunger of the SOUL…goes UNFED.
Love is the only food for the soul. Can I learn to love me?

Mother Earth's Mantra...

If you don't know the water...how will you find the stream?

I am at the core of the depth of your pain
I understand the yearning to love you need to regain.

Lift the veil that keeps you from seeing
My unconditional LOVE in the core of your BEING.

Let my love re-enter your heart
Swelling, surging, presenting a brand-new start.

Only LOVE helps to navigate the separateness that began at birth.
Come back home to me, the essence, your Divine SELF- WORTH.

Everything matters but nothing is vital
In the sojourn of the Divine you are all entitled.

Be part of my community of Earthly beings
Receive the gift of Heavenly Wings.

Use my Mantra, repeat it often
Feel your light beginning to soften.

If you don't know the water, how will you find the stream.
It is the flow of consciousness creating reality from the dream.

Declaration of Love

Even before the dawn, I am awake.
My senses are filled with anticipation for the night approaching
when we will be together again.
Why would one sleep when the waking moments are better than a
dream?

To be real with someone, so alive, so engaged
in a love continually perpetuating itself.
Rolling over itself, embracing us like waves
lapping at the shoreline.

We are cleansed with Love,
sometimes rocked with passion,
other times, soothed and caressed.

No sense of reason will be salvaged now…
no fear will survive under the bright shining light of your love.
Surrender my only option,
I exhale with a great sense of relief in your embrace.

The Path to Heaven on Earth

Here is your road map to Heaven on Earth,
Here is your path laid out for you.
Here is the only thing you have to focus on to get there.
Here is the way to be with God.

Simple…Simple?

You must focus on three areas:
the body, mind, and spirit,
because all three must arrive together.
They are after all one and the same.

One package with three gifts in it.
Pay close attention to each of these,
I will call them terms.

They are words that have meaning…
like all words, they represent something.
The body is your Sacred Temple, the mind your Master and Spirit is
the essence of God. God does not interfere unless invited. That fact is
irrefutable.

God gave us FREE WILL, that means FREE, without restriction,
without qualification, without restraint. All the more reason whywe
must be diligent with our intention.

We have every right to destroy ourselves, God will allow you to do
that…intervention will only come if we ask for help and forgiveness.
You can literally treat your body with disdain, feed it full of garbage,

drive it to distraction, pleasure it until you are empty, whip it into shape, push it to its limits. If it is your desire to test the body's endurance, go for it…no one…not even God will stop you.

However, your body is your Sacred Temple. It houses your Divine Energy. What is it you are trying to prove? How strong you are, how resilient you are, how powerful you are? Of course, you are all these things, God has already decreed that, you are made in his image. You have been given all of this already.

There is nothing to prove, nothing you cannot do. You are powerful beyond your wildest imagination. Everything you need is already here, already been placed in your path.

God knows exactly what you need…to be at one with your body, mind and spirit.

God gave all of us FREE WILL. The mind is the Master. The mind will take you to many places. You can go wherever you would like. If left unchecked, the mind will wander through the desert of wasteful and useless thoughts forever. You must choose where the mind goes and where it doesn't go.

Everything you have seen, read or experienced is now part of your mind and your body's memory, most of it totally unconscious. Some of this information is worthless at best. Movies, television, magazines, some books, pictures, the things that draw our attention can negatively affect our body, mind and spirit.

All unconscious information is disruptive. We must choose proactively, food for the spiritual, in the same way we feed the body food, we feed the spirit food through interest in whatever draws our attention. We must learn to be impeccable when it comes to that information. Any information that diminishes our human capacity to love, or takes away our power to make decisions, that does not align us with our highest SELF, is going to literally diminish our light, dull our focus, sap our energy, and eventually, make us completely unaware of our spiritual essence.

The innocence of children is a good place to understand that concept. They have FREE WILL until someone teaches them they don't. The energy of that FREE WILL is boundless, eternal, and GOD driven.

God gave us all FREE WILL. Spirit is the essence of our being, the conscious energy that makes up all of life. God is in the driver's seat, the mover of energy, the motivation, and the determination. But the intention is ours. What we want to create in our lives is ours to choose. Once that purpose of life is set, God will help move us toward our goals.

If you are quiet and listen, your direction will be crystal clear. Will you listen to the will of GOD, singing your praises, helping make your decisions when you are unsure? Will you surrender to God your FREE WILL and turn your body and mind over to God to direct your path? Letting go of the need to control is our most challenging obstacle. God will not take over the helm without a direct and heartfelt invitation. When you learn to let go and let God be the director of your life, watch your life change. Watch it, and let yourself become a child of GOD.

These three areas of our lives all work in conjunction with each other. They are not separate, they are ONE.

You cannot care for the body without conscious intention to appreciate, embrace, and have compassion for your physical experience here on

Earth. You must feed it natural whole food, drink pure water, get plenty of rest, move your body in a way that is balanced, compassionate, and conscious...always moving yourself toward wholeness.

You must be the Master of your own mind, taming the energy through still sitting, contemplation, and meditation. Focus on beauty, focus on Love, focus on your Higher SELF.

The body is physical, yes, but your body is the sacred temple that houses your spiritual essence. Just know that; be aware of that concept. That is how you will connect with the world and the people around you. Without awareness of that spiritually, you become cynical, resentful, jealous, and separate from your fellow humans. You could become lethargic, uncaring, and lose your innate capacity for deep Love...which is your Divine gift.

Pretty simple, don't you think? Be conscious of each and feed them all well. Whet their appetites with healthy well-balanced awareness; they can become insatiable. Each one must have a balanced diet of nutritious food, information, and an appreciation for SELF- satisfaction.

Heaven on Earth awaits those who make a conscious effort to be with their Divine presence. The Divine is all powerful, all forgiving, all compassionate. All you have to do is express an interest in being the child, it's that simple.

Set your intention for connection with the Divine, chart your course, and SAIL to Heaven on Earth in God's loving stream of consciousness.

Take these words into your heart and feast yourself on God's Eternal Love.

The Real World

In dreams I am alone, wandering seemingly aimlessly,
across terrains unfamiliar...
yet somehow my soul has knowledge of this journey.

As I am nudged from slumber, life coming clearly into view,
I awaken to your presence.
The warmth, the smell of you, your soft caress.

You awaken also, you reach for me, your awareness
of me, as you come back from the dreams of the night, filling you.

I can sense the leaving of our singleness, only to meld back
in the joined life we have consciously chosen to walk together.

The blanket of your love covers me, softly,
as I become aware of the gift of another day stretching out before me,
waiting to be experienced.

Passion without warning stirs us together,
the breath quickens, our bodies begin their dance of love
that we have come to know so well.
Just before entering the world of obligation and purpose
we are swept away into each other,
this place of no boundaries, where I am you and you are me.
One body playing a musical symphony, that is both serene and stormy,
with peaks and valleys moving over mountainous terrain,
swimming in the deep waters of Mother Earth's wet juicy land of erotic
dreams.

As the sun appears over the horizon, the day dawning.

We make ourselves ready to enter the Unreal world,

with full knowledge and commitment to our chosen separate lives.

Acutely aware of the secret life we share always beating, throbbing,

pulsing through us, as we anticipate throughout the day,

the reuniting of body and soul when the sun sets.

Nature

I sit here in the midst of nature.
My tent is parked in your back yard.

At home, here praising God with every breath.
Like the birds, squirrels, and who knows what else,
I too, am God's little creature.

I too struggle for survival, scratching out my subsistence,
creating my nest home, giving praise and thankfulness
to my ability to live with my spirit alive and well…intact.

You let me come here. You didn't even laugh when I suggested this
wild, foolish notion of spending time here encircled with trees in your
living room of God, instead you walked the back yard to choose the
spot for the tent to be…quoting Carlos Castaneda: "It is not safe to sit
in the middle of the energy, it will be too strong," you said…sit on the
outskirts.

And so, you carefully chose a SAFE place for me to be.

What a great job you did, and I appreciate you taking my inner child
under your wing, as she revisits the missed opportunities in youth to
explore her wild woman energy.

How is it, a man understands these yearnings.

Perhaps men have the same yearnings for their wild man to live and
thrive.

Perhaps we are living our dreams sharing our wildness and wilderness, those places left untouched in our psyche, with each other.

Me riding with you on your motorcycle, you doing yoga, me studying scripture, attending Adoration, you getting bodywork.
How did God choose you for me, how did he find you,
this perfect man for my perfect woman.
How did he know exactly what I needed?
Maybe he heard me crying, heard my moans,
like the moaning of a whale underwater.
Unable to make sense of this journey alone but trying to find ways to make it work.
Trying everything to find a way to make it work.
Not wanting to give up, not wanting to surrender before the discovery of what was in store for me presented itself.

And then you arrived…with the clarity of a crystal, you arrived. I saw forever in your eyes, I saw forever in your heart, saw your amazing insights into God.

I lived before; I thrive now. The difference is you.

Enter the Divine

Sitting in the cool early morning breeze,
my thoughts seem to emanate in the rustle of the trees.
Somehow in my deepest being,
an awareness of my soul's learning.
Leaning to the right, to my busy doing side,
a relentless feeling of a roller coaster ride.
How is it that doing takes precedence over being?
That stillness is lost in the hustle, bustle, not seeing.
The connection with the soul's joyful journey,
Will have to start over, again and again, returning.
Over and over until the truth is finally heard,
Connection with the Divine is the final word.
No more running, in continual distraction,
with life only lived as a process of reaction.
When finally, after many lifetime lessons,
I have learned to say thank you for all those blessings.

Understanding the Divine was always in charge,
The ego stopped fighting a battle so large,
It took lifetimes and lifetimes of clearing karma,
To Enter the Divine porthole and the bliss of dharma.

The Art of Love

Staring at the crackling fire, I lose myself in warmth and light,
Watching the flickering of orange and yellow.
Stillness washes over me, my awareness turns to you, my love.
My inner artist begins to paint,
your lips, your body, even your breath, become vividly etched on my soul.
Each cell of my body remembering,
We searched for eons to find each other.
Do you remember that moment of recognition?
Even now we separate into our days and then come back together.
As we sleep our bodies tune themselves,
Our hearts finding one heartbeat, our breath finding one breath.
As the sun awakens a new day,
We find ourselves making love without restraint, without inhibition washing clean with huge red stokes.
Passion the only paint on the canvas now.
No body, no mind, only our spirits seeking resolution, connection, release.
The canvas is washed clean, waiting for the next brush stroke creating a new day together.
Using the entire rainbow for a palate,
Painting a life inspired by love, moved by passion, entraining two hearts.

The Vibration of Humanity

The soundtrack of life, vibrating sound into matter,
Manifesting, creating all of life.

Every living being playing their part in the symphony,
Listen intently to that cacophony of sounds...

The harmonies, the discord, the screeching, and screaming cries,
The terror, the pain, raw emotion, aggression,
And at the same time, joy, laughter, all of life mating, coupling,
The spirit at play in wild ecstasy,
And God conducting it all.

All of this happening simultaneously,
God's orchestra,
God's voice speaking through every living creature.

Will you listen?
Really listen, as the voice of humanity cries out?
Be attentive to the conductor,
The concerto of love is written.
The orchestra of God is playing.
Do you know your part?

Use Loving, compassionate, encouraging words,
Keep your eye on the CONDUCTOR.
Your only reliable sheet music is written straight from your HEART.

AND PLAY ON....

The Sweetness in Life

Dichotomies, Anomalies, Astrological projections.
Lives all stressed fear and rejections.
What happens when humans confronted by change,
Taking on life, trying to rearrange.

Placing control and reinforcement
On the law of gravity's counter endorsement.
Surrender is the only answer,
Intuition is the life force…the dancer.

The sense that movement of a higher direction
Must replace the mirror of our old reflection.
Take a risk, step out on that limb,
Pretend you are back on the jungle gym.

Playing at life as if you were the goal,
Not letting responsibility take such a toll.
Remember that lighthearted child,
Before heaviness extracted the wild.

Sensation of pleasure and bliss,
We once found in the soft sweetness of a first Kiss.

Awake, Alert, Alive

2013 – present

Acceptance

The act of consenting to accept
Something given as a gift.
To see life presented with the concept
Of a Divine energy designed to lift

Humanity in all its frailties and flaws,
Taking a higher road than its current place.
Where being accepted, injected with laws,
Human behavior is a fast-paced race.

Humanness requires a moral ethic,
Compassion, kindness, family ties,
A global view, our connection kinetic,
A work of art, movement affecting all lives.

What will it take to understand...?
Our bond, our connection, cannot be broken.
Seeing the world as one continuous land
With many languages being spoken.

We may not comprehend another's words
Or differ in looks from culture to culture,
But to think of humans as different is absurd,
God designed the perfect human sculpture.

All of us come from the very same mold,
A system with its basic intention perfect,
No amount of money or gold
Will ever duplicate or totally affect

The evolution of mankind as we travel
This journey through mystical space,
Our willingness helping us unravel
God's reason for the gift in the first place.

Alone

I came here alone
Although not without help
As if a cyclone
Swirling, sent me out with a yelp.

From my cozy existence
The warmth of a womb
I arrived with resistance
From the quiet of a tomb.

No idea what to expect,
Taking it all in
I must admit at times I regret
Leaving the quiet safety within.

Now, of course, I see the reason
Behind my inability to stay.
Still I yearn with every season
Looking for a way.

To find a quiet still place
Going back to the world I remember
Getting out of the race
An opportunity to surrender.

Releasing all tension
The negativity I have taken on
Focusing my attention
Before I come upon

The next phase on the road I travel
Challenging me to awaken
Seeking to unravel
My inner voice that lies forsaken.

The part of me that knows
There is no need to worry
Perhaps I came to write prose
In any case there is no hurry.

Being a Woman

Being a woman is challenging for sure
Nobody told me or gave a clue.
At first my Mother's life was the lure
But it didn't take long before I knew.

Her path was not destined to be mine
Her sorrows I could not bear,
It would take more to define
Much more to prepare.

The path I had chosen
With so much to learn
I could not stay frozen
My heart trying to discern.

What was real
What was fake
What to feel
What to forsake.

All these choices demanding action
Not knowing what direction to take
Looking simply for satisfaction
With an entire lifetime at stake.

Going inward for resolution
Seeking Divine intervention
Desperate to make some contribution
Holding onto the highest intention.

Relying on the intuitive to nurture
The best outcome of all concerned
Looking toward the future
So much to be learned.

Being Here

When I am here
Whole and still
Feeling clear
Waiting until…

A larger picture
I begin to see
Without stricture
ME…totally FREE.

Unencumbered by rules
Energy without restraint
A box of new tools
New canvas to paint.

One step at a time
Letting the dance unfold.
Enter the sublime
New story waiting to be told.

Listen to your inner voice
Coming from the deeper part of you.
Your life, your choice
A transformation into:

Newly birthed awareness
From your light inside
Spiritual Fairness
Inner source no longer hides.

The gift of life
Not only physical
No more strife
Allowing in the Metaphysical.

Ideas, preposterous, so far out
At first, feeling like a stranger
An inner understanding, so true, so devout
As you become the changer.

Changing our existence
One step at a time
Through loving persistence
And an upward climb.

No need to worry
There is no finish line
No need to hurry
Infinity has plenty of time.

Deep Sleep

In the hallowed halls
Of a fitful slumber
I ponder the many recalls
Of my life, too many to number.

The mind has a need to remember
The scenes of my past
Lest I forget to dismember
The many missteps I have amassed.

Like being forced
To watch an old, outdated tv show
As if the only source
Were the mistakes I already know.

Changing the past is an impossible feat
That is a fact.
No action must be considered defeat
While dealing with the abstract.

To remember the past
Feeling it inconsistent
So as not to repeat
What seems so persistent.

Why is letting go
Moving on, so hard
Why the pace so slow
With a strange disregard.

For creating something new
More vibrant and alive
Not just moving through
A long dark night, trying simply to survive.

Taking a deep breath now
This too shall become the past.
The light of day will allow
A mere shadow left to cast.

Accepting is part of the struggle
Trying to understand our human condition.
As awake, or asleep we juggle
Until our lives begin a new rendition.

Definition of Euphoria

As in every aspect of what we call sanity,
Euphoria is no exception.
Happiness and self-confidence or a pathological vanity,
Sheer bliss or a deep deception.

Perspective must be considered,
Is the view from outside or in,
A euphoric state can be withered
If judged by ourselves or another as a sin.

We are all here to find our inner guide,
No one's judgement but your own has worth.
Many states of heart and mind will slide
Through our mind and body on this earth.

Judgement needn't be part of the picture,
We are all allowed to feel
All experiences allowed for the human creature.
It's not the feeling that disrupts the ideal.

Which feelings and how we react
Will either blow our cover
Or keep us intact
While we struggle to discover.

Is there a purpose for our energetic vessel?
Capable of such highs and lows,
Are we born of a breed incredibly special,
Or here to destroy all that we know.

The search and the answers are yours alone,
You have the right to build or destroy,
Your action and beliefs come from the unknown,
Until your future unfolds in misery or joy.

The state of your mind is the true motivator,
But the heart and consciousness are the Driver.
Unless they work together the ego becomes the perpetrator
And the heart becomes merely a survivor.

Heart and mind working as one
Can lead us down a different road.
One where euphoria and sadness together run,
The seeds you plant become the life you sow.

Do not fear the past, the future you see,
Both are an integral part of the learning,
Who you are and who you came to be
Will illuminate the life that needs discerning.

If you do not recognize your INNER being,
The euphoria and despair will be your only reality.
The truth is in the balance, the agreeing,
Our connection with intrinsic sensuality.

The head, the heart, the senses playing the same,
All an important part of the plan,
Creating Humanity, the name of the game.
When you finally get connected, God will become your biggest fan.

Each Day Has Value

Days are not to be wasted
They must be thoroughly chewed and tasted
Each Bite Savored
Being sure we haven't wavered

From our own individual Divine Path
Specifically chosen for your particular gift
Avoiding the wrath
That comes down heavy and swift

When you choose to deny
The power you were given
And waste the unending supply
Of Divine energy you were given

You can provide justice and peace to all
Letting your light be the guide
Hearing the call
No more backward slide

Engaging fully with the heart
As we reach out to touch others
Every day a brand-new start
Embracing all your sisters and brothers

Each Generation

In each generation,
There lies a gap.
A place of miscommunication,
A view, a wider map.
The difference is interpretation.

It begins with the innocence and purity of youth,
With a need to understand.
Seeking the more obvious truth,
Living life in the moment, unplanned.

Then Adolescence, a time of confusion,
With hormones raging,
Inability to draw logical conclusions,
Seeking connection but somehow instead disengaging.

Waiting for maturity to find us,
Never knowing the meaning of grown-up.
Trying not to make a fuss
Or let anyone get too close-up.

Before you know it, middle age
Has a way of sneaking up from behind.
Without realizing each day was the turn of another page,
Our entire life constantly redefined.

Each decade requires examination,
Without total clarity.
Sometimes passing by with quiet resignation,
And the vague sense of familiarity.

Before you know it a check called Social Security,
Gray hair, wrinkles and all.
Perhaps this is the definition of maturity,
But I rather believe it's just the call

To finally relax without worry,
No destination or plan of action.
Just a sidestep to life's flurry,
Being present without the distraction

Of life's busy TO DO LIST
Always in the forefront.
Allowing yourself the pleasure to resist
The need to DO, always on the hunt.

The single best message to leave behind
Is "relax" you're going to get there.
Give yourself time to unwind,
You have already paid your fare.

Your journey is never ending,
Energy cannot be destroyed,
No need to go on pretending,
Into the Infinite Universe you have been deployed.

You see there is no beginning and no end,
No need to worry where to start or where to finish,
What matters is what you intend,
Your light will never diminish.

Fear of Death

Do you hear death knocking at your door,
Say loudly, "you got no invitation."
Like a lion with a roar,
"You have a lousy reputation."

"What do you want?"
Speak with authority.
Break the detente.
Make your inner SELF the priority.

Death is seductive,
"You have nothing left to do," it said.
I say, "I still can be productive."
I knew I was being misled.

Many options lie in wait,
I don't even know them all.
The ability to create
Is in opening to the call.

The gifts we hold
Will be presented,
Becoming uncontrolled
When the inner child is represented.

She is the one who is facing extinction
Every day in the choices she makes,
She rides the wave of life with distinction,
Never seeing her lessons as mistakes.

Allowing life to be a co-creation,
Listening intently to the inner voice.
Sometimes needing more information,
Using her patience when making a choice.

Life is not a game
To be played with winners and losers,
With some prize to claim
Given to the abusers.

We are all on the same team,
The Captain is the Divine.
We are players in the dream,
Helping each other is the design.

No losers or winners,
Just one day at a time.
Every day we are beginners,
Reaching for the sublime.

Totally Free,
No worries or fears,
A place we all agree,
All doubts disappear.

First...Love Yourself

Love is not a feeling for one single person
But more an inner state of being.
Relationship, euphoria, worsen
Because the vision of self-love is true seeing.

A more extraordinary view of the world,
Connection made through the senses,
An open portal examining what is unfurled,
Without judgement, condemnation or offenses.

The view of what IS without demand,
Being honest and sincere in every situation.
Seeking the personal truth at hand,
Capable of authentic and purposeful participation.

What happens outside is out of your control.
Look inside, into your own reflective understanding,
Seeking personal truth always the goal,
Never allowing ego to do any reprimanding.

Your work, your vocation, mirrors your inner desires
And should reflect a strong belief system.
Body and mind coming together like two sticks creating inner fire,
Growing together without any resistance.

Mind/body connection reflects the spirit's will,
No contradictions, complete collaboration,
Strength and purpose instill
A heartfelt desire for inner communication.

Your journey begins with small steps,
Don't rush, let patience be your ride.
Forward movement, no regrets,
Use your heart as your guide.

Grace

Through Grace
I become whole.
Opening space,
Giving up control.

Learning to embrace
My inner soul.
Living without a trace,
Letting the Divine set the goal.

Learning to be free,
Set the world aside,
I'm learning to be ME,
Taking life in stride.

There is no greater glory,
Set aside expectation,
Living a truer story
Of Divine human creation.

Being in the silence
Instead of noisy chatter.
Giving into resilience,
And things that really matter.

Seeing life with Clarity,
Treat all humans with respect.
Speaking with sincerity,
Living life without regret.

Higher Learning

I am now earning my PhD,
Not quite developed yet
A class in "inner productivity"
With me as the boss, that's my safety net.

Getting fired for not doing your job
Is something I completely understand.
The notion to steal or rob,
But I saw employers who planned

To save money by lying about products.
Who also used intimidation and lying
To avoid paying a decent wage, really sucks.
Thinking they were funny or smart, but we knew why.

Keeping my mouth shut has never been my way,
Somehow the truth will seep past my lips,
Words slide out to betray,
Unjust and unfair practices slip

Out of my mouth without a warning,
So easily, I am taken by surprise,
Until the look on my boss's face forewarning,
Back into the unemployment line I surmise.

Oh well, some jobs are not worth the time,
No amount of money is likely to persevere,
When business becomes more about the bottom line
And less about the customers they serve.

One more job ended.
One more lesson learned.
One more class attended.
One more truth discerned.

Such is life and its evolution.
Seeking a place to be at peace.
One that strengthens motivation,
And allows the running and hiding to cease.

These days I don't regret speaking my mind,
I actually enjoy listening to my inner thoughts.
I no longer worry about what I might find,
Or telling the truth and getting caught.

Being fired is the least of my concerns.
Even if it happened, I will just move along,
So many new things to learn.
The score of life is written, I just sing the song.

Humanity as a Work of Art

What message can be said
To take the pain away.
What affirmation can we spread
To others, to make them want to stay.

We are sinking it seems in a deep abyss,
The darkness overtaking.
If I could present a truth in one wish,
We would all wake up and see the reality we're making.

Humans are the key to life and death,
All options are on the table.
Take the struggle to the Breath,
Misery is only one scenario.

Here is the question at hand,
The one only we are refusing to answer.
Can we collectively command.
Will we learn to share love or accept and spread the cancer.

Life and death are a delicate balance.
It's like we are sitting on a fence,
Waiting for some kind of compliance.
Watching from afar a battle that makes no sense.

It saddens me to think,
Through all these wars and devastation,
So little has changed as we continue to sink,
Every day another story, little hope for preservation.

Humanity is a gift from God and Mother Earth,
To prove we can love with a full heart.
We are failing the challenge to see human worth,
Humans are the work of God's Art.

In the Quiet

Who knew this quiet solitude
Would reveal all that IS?
I closed my eyes and the stars appear from out of nowhere.

The stillness unobservable from any place of engagement from the outside world.
The treasure arises from the darkness, revealing life out the depths.

What is in the void. It is life in its truest essence,
No need to question, guess or judge,
Just the purest bliss of unadulterated love and presence.

These moments of purity are the most precious of all,
Because they don't depend on doing anything
But simply being in the presence of life itself.

In the quiet stillness, peacefully,
I can access the very deepest recesses of my being.
There I encounter the bliss.

There I can come face to face, acknowledging with gratitude,
The ins and outs of life and the door that swings at will,
Bringing me to acceptance of both worlds
Simultaneously facing each other in sweet gratitude.

Thank you

Life's Double Edge Sword

In all that we do
And all that we are
One concept comes through
Shining like a brilliant star.

We can't call it good
We shouldn't call it bad
But if we understood
Our child would be more joyful and less sad.

We can all agree what goes up
Will also find its way down
Let's look at this close up
The explanation is sound.

Energy follows his own way
Moving each and every one
Seeking balance in every day
From morning to the setting sun.

The circle of life is like peeling an onion
Removing layer after layer
The yang and the yin
In the center's balance is the slayer.

Wielding a mighty sword
Slashing through untruth
As you sever the cord
Until all that's left is YOU.

In every situation
Every life event
Honesty without hesitation
Can help to circumvent.

Bottom line reveals who you really are
Coming from the Universe or perhaps a star
You traveled eons to appear
A very long journey from afar.

Use a sword, wield it like you mean it
Act as if you have a purpose
You don't know it all, admit it
Pretending you do is worthless.

Search for truth throughout your days
Don't ever give up
Never sacrifice your loving ways
To fill someone else's empty cup.

Love Yourself Beyond Reproach

"To love an illusion is to miss the point of love itself."
- Marilyn Morrison

I saw the tip of the ship like an iceberg,
Slowly descending into the cold water.
Shocking to see something so large as it began to submerge,
Stunned but detached, my eyes could not avert.

As it went down with a violent surge,
I was holding on like I needed the anchor.
Some old wound needing to purge,
Something possibly moored in my harbor.

Life is perplexing, seemingly without reason,
Listening can be painful.
A voice must be heard, even if it feels like treason,
Acknowledging even what is viewed as shameful.

But to not listen at all,
Would be the worst sin possible.
Like refusing to answer an important call,
Something in the psyche, both irrefutable and blameful.

Our sense of INNER justice is beyond reproach,
Never miss an opportunity.
Dreams can appear at times as a life coach,
To explore for the sake of UNITY.

I learned a sinking ship is not about doomsday,
It could be about letting go
Of some things we regret but never say,
Some past ideas releasing their fray.

Allowing courage and the ability to open
To a better understanding and our willingness,
The lighthouse in the distance as a beacon,
To release old wounds and the opportunity to witness,

Less resentment and guilt,
More joy and action,
In the life we have built,
Seeking knowledge of ourselves with greater
SATISFACTION.

My Little Friend Said to Me

It was like a confession: "I have ADHD."
Yes, I said, You have a lot of energy.
"It's something that happened to me."
Going through a lot has confused your synergy.

"I'm always going to be this way."
Maybe not, you do have choices.
Awareness of SELF today,
Can change your inner voices.

"I'm not sure I have control over my thoughts."
When you hear a voice saying you aren't good enough,
Something that makes you feel distraught,
Whatever your head says, stand up for yourself…get tough.

Don't put yourself in a negative hole,
Be positive about who you are,
Bad thoughts will take their toll,
Putting out the light of your INNER STAR.

Our Unfolding Lives

Our life unfolds
We stretch out
Reaching for the Untold
A story without

Imagination and joy
Is not worth telling
A story to employ
The wild self-compelling

Others to also reach
For the highest rung
Of the ladder, to teach
Both old and young

What it would mean
To allow the human gift
Stepping out of the routine
Asking Spirit to lift

Each of us willing to share
In our own time
As we become aware
Up the ladder we climb

A new understanding of mankind
In an elevated state
One our Creator designed
One the EGO will hate

Giving up control
Relaxing inside
Setting our goal
Letting spirit provide

A path to wander
Without restriction
Time to ponder
Without being conflicted

There is a Divine Order
Part of the plan
Life without borders
The way it began

Into Infinity
No restrictions
With anonymity
No contradictions

One human race
Joined together
Taking up space
By working altogether

Elegy:

A Poem of Serious Reflection, Typically a Lament for the Dead

I write to myself, to explain, to ruminate, to accept, to apologize, to reject, to release, to complain, to purge, to elevate, and to forgive myself for my own ignorance.

An elegy to myself, the part that has passed away. The part that no longer has bearing in my life. I cry to release the sadness, the longing, the hurt and anger. Let it go, says my heart, you don't have to be that anymore.

Life is simply birth and death continually moving in and out of an energetic field. You are caught in that field as it beautifully and purposefully takes you into its loving hands and tosses you around, until you can feel your light body in all its strength and release all that is heavy and holding you back. Like a baker tossing pizza dough in the air, making it thinner and thinner, shaking off the excess flour, for a perfect crust.

This elegy is for you, to see your spirit soar, lifting you higher and higher and then lightly touching the earth, enabling you to receive the next phase of the life you came to experience this time. You have been here many times before, always with the purpose of finding your truth; it comes in pieces, in lifetimes, so you can see the whole picture.

You would never be able to do that in one short lifetime, so it is spread out to help you get the whole picture. Like volumes of an epic novel, not just chapters, but complete novels, created to tell the story of you.

Of course, the end of each novel is where the understanding comes. This is where the beginning, middle, and end begin to make sense to the reader. This is the wisdom you take into your next lifetime. You are the reader, the interpreter, the lead actress/actor in your play, but you are not the entire novel.

You are simply each page, telling your story. The complete novel is your God SELF. So...right now, you are at the arrow in the map that says, "You Are Here."

Let's see where it goes from this point, as you continue with a deeper understanding of who you really are, based on your experience and understanding. You have been seeking this your entire life and in other lifetimes also. A new phase, a new beginning is about to flourish. Use your imagination and see what creation you can bring to this world that can help all of mankind grow.

Your gift is waiting to unfold, spread out over time and space, unleashed on the world without objection, reservation, or doubt. Just you being YOU is all you need to make this glorious event a happening and bring recognition to your true SELF.

The Breath in Me

Breathe me, through to my soul, so I can know I am alive,
Let my breath come in and out like waves, unceasing, undemanding.
Just letting me be, present, giving me space to open, to relax.

Breathe me when I have no energy to breathe for myself,
when life has taken my breathe away and left me listless and heavy.

Breathe me so I know in the stillness I am here, awake and my very
own breath is taking care of me, like a mother soothing a child, saying
"Don't worry little one, you are mine and I will make sure in those
times when your will is weak that you are taken care of, if you just let
go and surrender to me, you will survive this moment and come out
as if escaping a cocoon that has wrapped you until you were ready to
appear."

Feel the peace in the breathe, stay with the rhythm of life that I breath
into you. Feel the gentle rocking motion of the ocean waves, nurturing
and comforting your soul. You may feel like you are underwater now,
but do not fear, I, your breath, will help you to surface again so you can
relax in your confident nature.

Focus the breath in for a count of five, exhale for a count of five. The
rhythm will take you for a ride, a slow and easy trip inside. A few
moments of reprieve from your busy head, trying to find the answers.

Your answers are not up there, your head cannot feel, only the heart
can see and feel the real you. Let that real you step out of the shadows
to be seen by the whole Universe. Your magnificent light will shine
for all to see, you will feel it, the warm glow of your own essence. Be
present with that, it is all you need. Do not fear yourself, you were made

from the silken strand of DNA that your creator manifested. You were created in the image of God, how else could such beautiful humanity have come into being.

Grace will both lead and follow you....

The Poetic Force

Sometimes I want to write poetry, but the essence isn't there. My mind grapples with ideas, but there is no coherent flow.

I put it away, put it to bed, let it rest, no pressure. I wonder if the ideas have dried up and perhaps will not resurface. This thought makes me sad. I love to sit and let the words and ideas spill from my head as my heart is forcing up its deepest longings to mirror myself to mySELF.

In a day or so, I calm down, and it's back, severing the wall like a sword slashing through my mind to bring elegance back to my being through the written word.

What a magnificent feeling, to present the flow of spirit on paper, rocking words to and fro like a wave, bounding, crashing ashore and rolling right back out into the depths of the deepest sea with my soul in tow.

How is it that this small, yet so significant, motion can bring such joy to the heart? The miracle of energy that synchronizes heaven and earth, making them one and the same.

It may be just a moment in time, disappearing and reappearing without any agenda except to fulfill a wild dream of the heart to be totally engaged with its creator.

A merging of energy so powerful it shocks both the heart and mind into a place of bliss beyond words, beyond comprehension, beyond belief. And it is there that oneness feels complete and true.

As tears glisten in my eyes and roll down my cheeks, I can taste the ocean of life in each drop. And my thirst is quenched for this moment. The yearning satisfied, my soul reaching its highest connection to wordless space without definition.

This is all I seek, simple moments in time when my heart touches the face of God and all is well in the world. Gratitude surrounds me like a cloak of heaven gently embracing. Ahhhh!!!!

Home Again

Entering with trepidation, through the doorway into the outside world, always with a feeling of unsureness. The outside world holds so much energy, all of it swirls and sways, reaching each of us, moving us toward something unseen, with purpose.

Trying to know God's will is like reaching into a grab bag with an expectation of something awful happening and smiling with delight when you bring out something completely, unexpectedly, wonderful. The opposite can also happen, reaching in for something wonderful and discovering something has grabbed you by the hand and you cannot shake it off. It is biting you like a rabid dog that will not let go of you.

Expect the unexpected, for your soul and your ego have very different ideas about who you are, different directions for you to travel, very different highways, with different markers and signs for you to read. Misreading those signs can be fatal.

Keep in mind that the soul will always try to bring you home, home to truth and grace. The ego is trying to fill an empty space with whatever it can find to distract you. If you find your home inside, the ego will have to disappear. This is well known in many ancient philosophical writings; the ego is tenacious, jealous, and has an appetite that is voracious, to distract you from your SELF. Death of the ego is not to be feared, it is to be embraced. For until you free yourself from the egoic mind, you will have no peace, no connection with your true SELF.

Do not fear your ego, give it space to be…then see if what it is telling you is true. If the ego is filling your head, ask it to be quiet. Learn some technique for quieting the mind, for there is no freedom without recognizing who is in the driver's seat of your physical experience. It must be the REAL you, the you that lies beneath the surface. When you begin to live life from a peaceful inner experience, you find your home space.

Coming home is an acknowledgment of your spiritual health, your ability to let go and surrender yourself to your SELF. In this place you can recognize who you really are: an amazing, intuitive, creative, blissful being who came to LOVE and appreciate life. If for no other reason than just because you are aware that you are ALIVE.

The journey is long and treacherous, expect pitfalls and danger. Look out for the potholes and the misleading signs, be diligent with your awareness. Let your inner guidance take you HOME, your inner space where peace, openness, and all you will ever need is at your disposal. There is nothing to want, it is already there in the form of energy, bringing your highest SELF into alignment with the ALL THAT IS.

Looking Through the Eyes of my Child

When my inner child looks around, what she sees is so different than what my grown person sees. Two sets of eyes, each one closing so the other can fake truth.

The child's eyes hoping to see something she can believe in from her lost innocence, always wanting to fill an empty space where love is believable and apparent and forever. She had to create it by herself, with her own disillusioned past. And then the adult working for the sole purpose of distraction from the truth.

As the child grows, she sees, only what has been covered over in a lifetime of lies, deceit, disingenuous pastimes. What has an entire lifetime to show for itself, false ideals, a need to stretch the truth into something comprehensible.

No use, nothing matches, nothing feels coherent or connected.
There was that traumatic moment when the body disconnected from physical awareness. Why? What was the reason for it? Who stepped in and created this moment? What was accomplished by this deed? Release, one person releases and the other learns to hold on tight, tighter, and more tight.

An entire life of holding on for dear life, the strain, the energy used to turn off that part of me that is the woman who wanted what every woman wants, simply to love. Shut that down, that is not about to happen. Look instead at what every man wants, release, look for something more plausible in life, something possible, easier to attain.

So that is life, ...life looking to rid itself of a lifetime.
Nowhere to hide, nowhere to go, nowhere to run to...here I am.

It is not possible to hold any more. I must find a way to release. I know what it feels like to be a man. I know that so much better than I know my woman. Today I open my eyes and see my female self. She is beautiful, loving and whole. The past is the past. Like the arrow in the mall map, You Are Here.

Let's see how the woman untethered by the past travels the world. With sex and money out of the picture altogether, these are not the needs of my grown-up child.

The focus of the man is gone, he never existed anyway, he was the aperture into the abyss that became my relationship model. He was the figment of an imagination and uncontrollable urge...period.
My whole life guided by a drunken urge. Wow, that is a very special awareness because it reflects the truth of my relationship with my father. So be it...The truth will set you free, just face it and let it go.

The Lotus Unfolds

I dream in connection,
I feel that connection,
I yearn for connection in my waking,
I am committed to that connection, even in my sleep.

It is as total as my every cell, every thought,
every experience including the past, present, and future.

Understand all are a part of the bigger whole to accept, and embrace this very physical, mental, and spiritual aberration, this is what I am having for my morning nourishment today.

From this Earth, what we see is the not the whole story. When the lotus unfolds, the true story is revealed to us through knowing who we are.

We are an aberration of the spiritual concept of what it means to be human on Earth; we came from somewhere else, we don't know where. And we don't have to know.

To even grasp a small portion of this concept requires an immense faith and trust in the process without even knowing what that process is...

One part I do know is that I am one small cog in the wheel of evolution. Without my cog this wheel will not function according to the higher plan. I am important.

Waking to this importance, accepting this gift and doing my small part in the human experience on Earth is simply letting go, releasing into the energy of the Whole. Taking my place in the wheel of life.

This is what the decade of 70 years is for me.

The gift is being realized, accepted, and most importantly, appreciated.

Let the Divine Games Begin,

The Lotus is unfolding.

Writing in My Sleep

I wrote poetry in my sleep last night,
I remember it was beautiful, thought provoking, heartfelt prose.

This morning it's gone, the feeling remains but the words are lost to the Universe, disappeared like smoke trailing off and vaporizing into thin air.

Are they still there, floating around somewhere looking for a place to land and be spoken? My contribution is small, fleeting, almost beyond my own awareness, but it is there, written somewhere in the great cosmic energy field.

My personal dream for peace on the planet, I send it out to reach beyond words, beyond my imagination, to the energy that can come together with all our thoughts of peace and Make It Real on Earth.

Some say, impossible. Some cannot fathom peace on Earth. I cannot fathom the Earth without peace. I know there is a way, because I found peace in my own heart; if it is possible for me, a mere mortal, to experience peace, even if fleeting, then I know it can happen for everyone.

Pick up all your little pieces of peace and with your hands fold it together, knead it together in a ball and throw it out for the whole world. Pick up the ball like you were throwing out the first pitch at the World Series, getting ready for the game to begin. Let us have our own World Series; let the World Series of Peace begin.

Solitary Moments for Viewing Only from the Single Eye

A look around, a walk about through the inner terrain.
Not looking for anything special, just viewing the landscape.
Like Sherlock Holmes with his spy glass, looking to magnify all the parts simply to inspect. There is a moment when I become both the inspector and the inspection - checking for overflow or deficient flow.

At first, I seem like an alien to myself, different from my waking awareness. The nightly walkabouts are a way to connect with the deeper side of who I am, the aspects created in me before I could think about who I am. Just allowing myself to be present with my own energy field. Some very interesting stuff makes an appearance.

I am one small cog in the wheel of evolution in this human experience. Walking up to the immense importance of accepting this gift and doing my small part in moving the understanding of our humanity forward. I simply release the ideas of who I am and allow myself to sink into the energy of the whole.

This is what the decade of the 70s is all about for me. The Gift realized, no wonder I have been waiting for this decade. The understanding of bringing the heart, mind, and body together for the fullest experience of being human without leaving any aspect behind.

I write about Spirit as far as my understanding can reach today, sometimes feeling like I am not here, physically disconnected, dizzy, and ungrounded. So I do my yoga and Tai Chi to bring myself back to myself, helping to ground my energy and reestablish my connection with

Mother Earth. Each aspect of our humanness must be fed, nourished so we can understand our human experience fully, and live life to our fullest capacity. There is more to this human thing than meets the eye... of that I am completely sure.

While I Awake

A night of stirrings and dreams,
My waking memory barely remembers.

Somehow the psyche worked it out
and I woke to a day cooler and crisper than any previous memory.
A new day unequaled in the past,
A day with no promises to keep or obligations to pay,
Just the shadowed sun casting light on freshly planted winter flowers,
and a stone Buddha's broad smiling statue sharing the view from my
little garden.

Age has mellowed and rounded my edges,
Giving me a smoother, fuller feeling of life in each day,
Not a day of things to do, but more, another day, just To Be Me.

The Dreams

Where do dreams come from, the psyche working out imbalances? Showing up as if a movie created, directed, and starred in by me. Short, to the point, so much so that it seems something is left out. The commercials are absent, no fluff, only the facts ma'am. Dreams can seem disjointed, unrealistic, and show us things that our logical mind cannot comprehend. Good...

This helps me to sort through physical, emotional, and spiritual pieces of myself, allowing for adjustments and corrections in my energetic field, letting my unconscious muse walk through the contradictions of my day.

My dreams take pieces and parts of my consciousness and unconsciousness to bring together two seemingly different worlds, to give me a closer look at how they partner when I am free to explore without my ego getting in the way.

I am hungry for the information that the night brings; many mornings I want to continue my inner focus without having to deal with the outside world. I long to know my Inner self more completely. To me this is where, in those conscious moments, we understand something truly amazing about our experience here on Earth.

I don't want to miss a thing.

A Prayer for My Body

What is it you want from me?
How can I help you just Be?
All this time trying everything,
Yoga, Tai Chi, upside down in the yoga swing.

You'd think I would be more familiar,
But still I have days when I feel peculiar.
Out of whack, out of sync,
Disconnected like the missing link.

A knowledge I am sure I hold,
Something in me left untold.
Still here I am, every year older,
My inner voice speaks up, "Haven't you told her?"

There is nothing you need to do
To know the inner you…
The present moment is the key
That will unlock the entire mystery.

There is a Place

There is a place I disappear into in the wee early morning hours, after my body has had its rest and my mind has emptied itself. A place that is so intrinsically ME, I don't even recognize myself and yet it is a place where my mind tries to ask questions, but the questions have no need for answers. A place where the body just wants to feel, but it seems there is no need for feelings either.

This place feels both empty and full. A place where the vastness is so complete, I don't know if I am at home or so far away, there is no such thing as a home. And yet, I am aware for a split second that I am THERE. But still don't remember where THERE actually IS.
I do know I have been there before I was form or intellect or body or anything that can be described with a word.

I feel the formlessness. It is the beginning, when I was a dream about to come to life as this Earth understands life. Now I am the dream again, the time traveler, the mystic, the real and the unreal coming together to stare at each other, as if neither were important nor have any consequence at all. Just simply the great IS-ness of all that is possible. In this great void of possibilities, I release my fears; they lift off of me like taking off a heavy coat and revealing the true nakedness of SELF for all to see.

Look at me, look at me, look at my beautiful nothingness and if you don't see me, look at my beautiful invisible SELF. This is my SELFIE portrait for 2014:

I am a landscape, a moon lit night.
I am the Grand Canyon, the great hole in the earth.

I am a baby's smile, I am the open air.

I am all this and more and I am nothing…NO THING NESS.

I am the energy of the ages, still waiting for form.

I am the slow process of creation reinventing itself over and over again.

Turn your eyes upward. You are that also.

It is GOD making something out of nothing and then turning it back into nothing once again.

The beautiful process of creation continually inventing itself.

This is THE PLACE where it all happens, nowhere and everywhere in a split second.

Relationships

Every relationship is a creative endeavor,
How long it last depends.
Some last a day, some forever,
With each person allowed to defend

Their physical space
Without changing who they are.
Not having to replace,
Or reach outside themselves too far

To please the other.
Losing their own direction,
Careful not to smother,
Or seek in others...perfection.

Perfection is programed into
The human connection.
Above, beyond, and through,
We seek ourselves through introspection,
Not another's point of view.

Skeletons in the Closet

A Question: What is the best way
To handle the skeletons in the closet?
Do we invite them out to play?
Or bar the door and lock it.

Like it or not they come out in dreams,
Not subject to the same physical constraints.
Skeletons move around by other means,
It would seem they have something to communicate.

Open the door to the darkness.
Do not be afraid of what it contains.
There are answers looming in the abyss,
The equilibrium must be maintained.

Ask the most daring questions.
Sit in the quiet opening,
Answers bring joy releasing tension.
You'll begin to see yourself more clearly...noticing.

Your inner life affects your outer life
In ways we cannot imagine.
A closer look at areas of strife,
The closet becomes the doorway to a mansion.

Many rooms, many possibilities,
Each with new awareness.
More options, more availabilities,
Leaving behind feelings of unfairness.

Launch yourself into a Universe,
The one inside only you can create.
Surrender yourself, immerse,
You were born perfect, it's your fate.

Social Ambiguity:

Doubtfulness or uncertainty of meaning or intention

Caught up, clustered together
Without reason or intention.
Any excuse for a get-together,
Social Ambiguity needs an intervention.

Formulate your own ideas,
Don't accept the norm.
There is no real panacea
In learning to conform.

Your own inner voice
Has the answers you need.
Listen intently, find reason to rejoice,
This is the only way to succeed.

Be still, let the silence speak,
It will take some reflection.
Each one of us is unique,
Look inside for your direction.

No one else has the answers
To the questions you need to ask.
Choreograph your own dancer,
Remove your old mask.

No need to hide behind
Someone else's truth.
Reflection helps you redefine
The qualities of your youth.

Innocence is your redeemer,
Love is the mirror.
Raising your self-esteem
As your life becomes clearer.

Learn what your child knows,
So when you are unsure,
Inner guidance can help you grow,
With a voice that's true and pure.

Struggle Can Be Growth

Learning how to struggle
How to win the fight.
All parts of us juggling,
Appearing out of nowhere; INSIGHT!

Learning, Growing, Understanding,
Then peeling the onion to provide
The answers that once came naturally expanding,
Using intuition and guidance from inside.

Amazing, letting life turn us inside out,
Only to reveal a deeper meaning,
Once we realize we cannot live without
The truest love, we can begin learning,

Trusting in something of a higher form
Has the answers we desire.
No longer needing to perform,
It's not THINGS we need to acquire.

The state of loving reception
Relieves all inner tension.
Guiding the heart into perception,
Elevating humans to a higher dimension.

A place where turmoil and unrest
No longer exist within,
A place where love is free to express,
Allowing life to truly begin.

The Beauty Within

In all this beautiful world
Only the human being
Is empowered to unfurl
Spreading Love and freeing

Transforming, transporting
Hate and fear
To kindness and love importing
To make it crystal clear

This is why we are all here
To ensure life's generous flow,
Each of us sincere
Learning how to show

Respect and goodness for all
Give yourself without reservation
You will hear the call
To pass your love to the next generation

The Christmas Tree Effect

What if our cells were tiny lights,
Shining together, creating one glow.
Each one recognizing its perfect right,
Within its system to know.

The vital importance of each cell,
Allowing its host to run full power.
As days passed, some lights fell,
No one knows the exact hour.

The power failure began,
It was a slow insidious fall,
We long to recover that feeling again.
Looking back trying to recall,

How the Bliss of Being left our side,
Sneaking away without our awareness.
We began a long and lonely ride,
Traveling into the wilderness.

As our Tree of Life loses light one by one,
Diminishing our ability to see,
The lights fail, all is done.
Unable to live with our lifeless tree.

Awakening is part of the Life Plan,
When we stray so far we forget,
How a once magnificent creature began,
Turning so easily to a life of regret.

The light had disappeared as I wiped my teary eyes,
I see the problem clear, there is nowhere to go,
My inner child forced to wear a disguise.
With playtime all but gone, the world would only show-

Deception and struggle were all it could teach her,
But it couldn't replace a deeper yearning.
She needed to touch her inner features,
To keep the Home Lights brightly burning.

So we sat in stillness for a while together,
My inner child and me.
Mulling over the path we weathered,
Trying to ignite and re-light our tree.

We had to agree on certain things,
But argued about how we arrived,
Behaving like two birds testing their wings,
Finally agreeing to a miracle...we both survived.

Now we travel a single road,
No longer opposing each other's force.
We broke the emotional, intellectual code,
My child and I speak now with one voice.

There is time to work, and time to play,
Each must be respected.
Making time in each day,
To allow the child and adult their individual perspective.

This is how I grew to understand,
All aspects of me are important.

Life in balance, all lights are in demand,
To make life work so no part of me lies dormant.

A full expression, "being lit like a tree,"
Is what I want for Christmas this year.
Perhaps you also are wishing like me,
A "lit up TREE" with NO fear.

The Gift of Motherhood

All that is deep,
The truest of love,
All a woman can reap,
Picture a soaring Dove.

A mother's body does
What it must do,
Takes away all that was,
Creating a world anew.

Not only for the child,
But for herself too.
Where there was quiet, now wild,
Every day exciting as you grew.

Life will never be the same
With this new source of love,
Onto the planet came,
Sent, I am sure, from Heaven above.

Arriving from the security of the womb,
Not to possess or own,
A mother and child in full bloom,
From this moment neither will be alone.

The connection is complete,
Two hearts create a bond.
Words would only deplete
A feeling reaching far beyond

This physical place,
Cannot understand
Two hearts joined in the inner space,
Exactly as planned.

Today I thank the beautiful souls
Who allowed me to be their Mother,
We each had our roles.
Grateful you chose me and no other.

The "I Am" Presence

Each of us as Humans have an "I Am" Presence,
A notion of our beginning to our end,
Not a stagnant resonance —
But a clearly stated message we send.

As we grow through Childhood, adolescence, and adulthood,
This "I AM" changes every day.
Some of it conscious and understood,
Other parts more elusive I'll say.

Our inner child, alive and well at all stages,
Is still running the show.
We might feel safe and loved or in cages,
Or we might not even know.

Wounded and afraid, the child may not speak,
Simply acting out our earlier retreat.
In anger and hurt the energy will leak,
Shocked and surprised, these patterns will repeat.

A wounded child has no choice,
Energy must find an outlet.
If recognition cannot provide a voice —
Behaviors will lead to outrage and regret.

Your "I Am" can be the answer
To questions about how you handle
Life's difficult situations when they register,
Alarm, fear, or sadness, don't coddle,

Speak to your child as an adult,
In a way that is compassionate and caring.
You might be surprised when you consult
With the younger part of yourself by asking.

Your logical self may think it is silly,
But if the way you behave eludes even you,
Take your insecurities to your inner ally,
Work through to find what is authentically true.

Together all problems have solutions
Your inner child can help resolve,
Bringing understanding and resolutions,
Know your Inner SELF, it is your birthright to EVOLVE.

The Inevitability of Change

Change has inevitable wisdom,
Nature doesn't resist or fight.
More like looking through a prism
Into shadows of days and nights.

Change is a constant force,
More something to count on than ignore.
Arriving straight from Source,
Not to destroy, but to help restore

The order of the Universe,
While working to maintain,
With amazing perseverance,
Helping life sustain

An evolutionary dimension,
Indestructible as it moves all life.
Conscious in its intention,
Order and purpose without strife.

If we could see this movement
As a Divine interaction,
Our stress levels would see vast improvement,
All of life viewed as a coming attraction.

The Mind Will Take You There

Opening minds, awakening,
Rubbing sleep from the eyes.
There is no mistaking
Difference between truth and lies.

We were undercover,
We did not know
Our need to love one another
Must continue to grow.

No messing up this time around,
With the help of each other.
We heard the blasting sound,
Bringing us out of cover.

The Untruth will fade away,
We will release ourselves from hate.
All the signs point to today.
We are ready, we won't be late.

If we can carry the torch of love,
Passing it to all who come,
Changing what is below and above,
Spreading Peace on Earth to
............EVERYONE.

The Night

Why is an event
Swimming in my mind,
Old memories lament
Some misstep, crime?

Committed without knowing,
Without even consent,
Not even showing
The sense to repent.

Ancient history
On my inner screen,
Some big mystery
Lying in between.

Wake and sleep showing up
Behind my eyelids,
A reflection close-up,
My sleep forbids.

Shadows in the night,
An old place and time.
I had taken flight,
Leaving my sleep sublime.

Into a porthole of the past,
Somehow I set sail,
Put up my mast,
Showing me in great detail

Some grievance from my youth.
A space on my timeline,
A deep-seated truth,
trying to redefine.

I'm tired I say,
why must I travel
so far away,
Trying to unravel

Or find some meaning,
In such a distant place.
It seems demeaning,
Trying to retrace

A misspent youth,
Instead of enjoying
A good night's sleep,
RUMINATING IS SO ANNOYING.

The Storm of Illumination

The storm ravaged the trees,
I watched it and it ravaged me.
The calm after the storm was brutal,
fighting my way through the silent futile.
No distractions, no power, lines torn down,
I hold on tight, my insides jittery, swirling around.
Opportunity for more inner space coming along,
Like music with no words to fill up the song.
Deafening silence intrudes in my world,
The deep pain of unexplored passion twirled,
It hurts, it aches, feels like a hole,
Useless ruminating trying to fill my soul
I would have thought it was about
Something I was having to do without.
But no that is not the reason,
It all boils down to personal treason.
I learned somewhere to fight the truth of ME,
Not giving my true self the right to be free.
Locking passion and purpose away in the dark,
Afraid of a landscape both barren and stark.
Waiting for the future to simply appear,
Praying to the wind to release the fear.
Fear of failure, fear of success,
The fear of not finding a place to rest.
At the same time, wanting more out of life,
Something missing that cuts like a knife.
By the fourth day, a realization hits hard and swift,
Abundance of life is an immeasurable gift.

It's not the emptiness that brings up my fear,
It is the illumination of my soul making it crystal clear.
To hold myself back takes more out of me,
Than allowing my inner Self to just BE.

The Ups and Downs of Life

Where is the level when you need it,
How to solidify the balance
When you can't manage the up and down with wit,
Seems words are no match for the inner dance.

Hard to justify or even accept,
When one day is glorious
While the next, I wept,
And life becomes laborious.

Heavy challenges my higher aspirations,
As I drop like mercury in a thermometer,
What are the implications,
The inner brakes causing a sharp drop on the speedometer.

Nothing within my control today,
Perhaps tomorrow will be brighter.
I might coax, or even sway,
Convincing my inner fighter

To drop the pretense, Let the mask fall away,
Removing the shadow that makes no sense,
So my inner child can come out to play.

Life is too short,
I must figure this out.
Perhaps I could deport or at least report
Whatever seems to cause me to doubt,

Or even find the reason I am here,
Before it's too late.
I must learn to steer,
And guide my inner fate.

So in the next life
I won't mind returning,
Perhaps with less strife,
And a vague recollection of this life's learning.

What's Happening

What's happening on this small planet Earth
That's making us all so crazy.
We have lost any sense of our own self-worth,
And I believe this is making us lazy.

We work, we work, we work ourselves to distraction,
Struggling for money and position.
We work so much without satisfaction,
Without asking what we value in our own action.

The scope and outreach of our understanding,
Allowing incorporation of all beings on Earth
Into our awareness by demanding
Each one of us discover our personal worth.

It's not about money or power,
But how much we are willing
To work every single hour,
Feeling our own personal growth can be thrilling.

To grow ourselves and share with others
The path of our unique experience,
Encouraging others to broaden their borders,
Lifting each other to new levels of confidence.

When Love Brings You More Than You Bargained For

When you appear in my dreams,
A light, a forceful beam,
Love reflects both what I know
And shines light where I won't go.

If I could take back just one day,
It would be that day I knew you were going away.
Knowing we would not make it through,
Wondering why it didn't matter to you.

Something came between us,
Perhaps I always knew.
Something was unspoken,
I think it was the Truth.

Funny how life twists and turns,
I got over you, but I had to learn
It was really me I was looking for.
I discovered so much more.

How life gives and takes,
In the process, how the heart can ache.
A broken heart affirms its need,
You planted a deep and willing seed.

From that seed I grew and grew,
Now I want to say Thank You.
Love's expression continues to give
The experience it longs to live.

Open and accepting what has been placed
On my doorstep will not be erased.
And so it is I say all this to you
With love and a heart that can now speak the truth.

When Questions Arise

When questions arise,
It is a true sign,
Perhaps too much compromise,
Perhaps we have crossed a line.

At some point we may have lost
Our true SELF, fighting to survive.
Inner guidance says the cost
Was too high, we must revive.

Our Inner Child is sad and weeping,
We no longer have control.
Our life force slowly seeping
Into massive puddles of vitriol.

Without awareness, we allowed
Others to wear us down,
Surrounded by a dense, dark cloud,
A face with a permanent frown.

There is so much more to life,
So much more to live for.
Unchain yourself from the strife,
Open your happiness door.

Let the clouds part,
The sun will shine through.
You can hit the restart
And begin your life anew.

Who is Driving the Vehicle?

Who is driving your vehicle,
It's imperative that you know.
It might just be an old cycle
Of the past trying to show

What happens when you don't have the wheel,
When your intention isn't doing the driving?
Life can become surreal,
You never know where you will be arriving.

It's always best to set your intention first,
Something simple, I want to do what's best for me.
That way you won't be coerced
Or led down a path you cannot see,

Into something that cannot be reversed.
Life experience should be of your own making,
You can collaborate as you immerse
With others who are also waking.

Learn to give freely from your heart,
Without the need for taking.
Relying on inner strength to impart,
This way there will be no mistaking.

Your intentions will be seen as pure and obvious
To all who interact with you.
Your direction led only by Your conscious,
Reflecting what is deeply true.

The spirit that shines your inner light
Will guide your direction through the dark.
In case your path becomes unclear in the night,
There will be times when a question mark

Appears to clarify your journey,
To offer a change of direction,
Or simply supply a gurney,
Lifting you to a new direction.

Sinking you deeper and deeper
Into your gifts and truth,
Relaxed and confident, recognizing keepers,
Relentless in your pursuit.

At the end of the line,
Happiness and a heartfelt appreciation,
As you look back on your time
Here on Earth with gratification.

There is no more to ask from life
Than Divine guidance,
Through the perils and strife,
Acknowledge the gift of subsistence.

The absence of stressing
Over situations beyond our control,
And learning to accept the inner need that's pressing,
The heart to love as we become WHOLE.

You're Almost There

I heard an inner voice say, "You're Almost There."
At first it seemed like a voice from Another,
My logical male left brain replied, "Where?"
An odd response to the inner right brain Mother.

Two sides of a connected brain,
So utterly disconnected,
Impossible to enjoy each other's Reign.
Instead they argue, each ineffective.

Unable to see each other's point of view,
Refusing to listen when they disagree,
Exerting control, accepting nothing new,
Arguing over and over with no referee.

Here is Mother's answer straight from the Heart:

When you begin to understand
The arguments created in your own mind.
You will then comprehend
Your true destiny, you will find

Your future depends on your ability
To evolve in your human capacity,
To use LOVE as the driving utility.
Your gift is intrinsic, it's in your audacity

To imagine everyone, the entire world
Living up to their true potential,
Global humanity under one flag unfurled,
Standing for love, their only credential.

No race, religion or ethnic group
Will be left out in the cold,
Humanity will stand as one large Troop,
Moving forward out of the old,
Selfish needs cast aside.
Love is Universal, helping each other,
Accepting everyone into our human tribe,
Putting a smile on the face of Earth Mother.

I Meant To

I meant to tell you
How much I care.
I meant to, but withdrew.
I know it's unfair.

If I don't speak up,
You have to guess.
We'll never get close-up
If I don't express.

What holds me back,
I wish I knew.
Something I lack,
I must pursue.

A deeper look inside,
A reflection into,
Helping to provide
A more internal view.

Allow my heart to speak,
Not just my head,
Fear of being weak,
Find my strength instead.

My words are sincere,
Straight from my heart.
If my message is clear,
Perhaps we can start

A brand-new connection,
One that will last,
Built with affection,
Not mistakes from the past.

About the Author

Marilyn began writing poetry as a therapy of sorts. It started as a journaling process and then each journal entry turned into a poem of hope and sincere soul searching. As the years passed the poetry became a means of understanding herself and accepting her life as a struggle but also as a gift.

Printed in the United States
by Baker & Taylor Publisher Services